to Barbara

with our love

Bill & Jane

May 1993

Flowers in a Broken Pot (1986)

by Roy Herrick.

Only Remember Me

Only Remember Me

An Anthology of Grief and Love

SELECTED BY A. G. GUEST

Marshall Pickering
An Imprint of HarperCollins*Publishers*

Marshall Pickering is an Imprint of
HarperCollins*Religious*
Part of HarperCollins*Publishers*
77–85 Fulham Palace Road, London W6 8JB

First published in Great Britain
in 1993 by Marshall Pickering

1 2 3 4 5 6 7 8 9 10

A catalogue record for this book is
available from the British Library

ISBN 0 551 02745-2

Printed and bound in Great Britain by
HarperCollinsManufacturing Glasgow

For Roy

Where my caravan has rested,
Flowers I leave you on the grass.

Contents

Love Endures   82

Tender Leaves of Hope　　99

The Last Journey   *122*

Introduction

This book is about Grief. Its shadow touches most of us at some time or another. When it comes, it darkens everything. Only those who have experienced the pain of grief know the anguish and sense of isolation which it brings.

The poetry, lyrics and prose in this short anthology have not been selected to illustrate differing attitudes to grief, or as representative of particular periods, or for any other purely literary reason. Rather my hope is that those who at any time have suffered bereavement will be able to recognize in these pages some of the many and varied emotions to which their grief gave rise, and that those who still grieve may take comfort from the fact that others have passed in thought along the same road. The memory may still cause pain, but, in Thomas Campbell's words –

To live in hearts we leave behind
Is not to die

Then there are the friends of those who grieve. So often friends assume that the best way to help a person "get over" grief is to pretend not to notice it, and above all never to mention the loved one who has died. For the bereaved, however, the most important thing is that someone, anyone, and especially their friends, should understand how great is their loss and the distress that they feel. It may be that a gift of this book will enable a friend to show, in a small way, that he or she does understand, even though it is not always easy to express that understanding in words.

This book is also about Love. For there is no grief without love. And love can flower even in grief.

We that are left

I Did Not Think . . .

If I had thought thou couldst have died,
    I might not weep for thee;
But I forgot, when by thy side,
    That thou couldst mortal be:
It never through my mind had passed
    That time would e'er be o'er,
And I on thee should look my last,
    And thou shouldst smile no more . . .

CHARLES WOLFE
To Mary

By the River

I was tired
When we found the place,
The quiet place by the river,
Where the sun shines through the willows,
Dappling the dark water
With green and gold.

I thought:
This is the end, this is peace.
We will stay by the river;
We will listen to its soft music
And watch its deep flowing.
The whispering leaves will be silent,
The golden shadows will deepen,
The river will rise and caress us.
Gently it will rise and embrace us
And bear us away, together.

Joyfully
I turned to tell you these things.
But I was alone by the river.
A cold wind shivered the willows;
Slowly a leaf twisted down to the water
And was carried away.

ANNA MCMULLEN
in *New Britain*

If We Could Know

If we could know
Which of us, darling, would be the first to go
Who would be first to breast the swelling tide
And step alone upon the other side –
If we could know!

JULIA HARRIS MAY
If we could know

If you had known
When listening with her to the far-down moan
Of the white-selvaged and empurpled sea,
And rain came on that did not hinder talk,
Or damp your facile flashing gaiety
In turning home, despite the slow wet walk
By crooked ways, and over stiles of stone;
If you had known

You would lay roses
Fifty years thence, on her monument, that discloses
Its graying shape upon the luxuriant green;
Fifty years thence to an hour, by chance led there,
What might have moved you? – yea, had you foreseen
That on the tomb of the selfsame one, gone where
The dawn of every day is as the close is,
You would lay roses!

THOMAS HARDY

That First Day

I wish I could remember, that first day,
     First hour, first moment of your meeting me,
     If bright or dim the season, it might be
Summer or Winter for aught I can say;
So unrecorded did it slip away,
     So blind was I to see and to foresee,
     So dull to mark the budding of my tree
That would not blossom yet for many a May.
If only I could recollect it, such
     A day of days! I let it come and go
     As traceless as a thaw of bygone snow;
It seemed to mean so little, meant so much;
If only now I could recall that touch,
     First touch of hand in hand – Did one but know!

CHRISTINA ROSSETTI
A Pageant and Other Poems

The Last Rose of Summer

'Tis the last rose of summer
    Left blooming alone;
All her lovely companions
    Are faded and gone;
No flower of her kindred,
    No rose-bud is nigh,
To reflect back her blushes,
    Or give sigh for sigh . . .

THOMAS MOORE
Irish Melodies

House of Rest

Now all the world she knew is dead
    In this small room she lives her days
The wash-hand stand and single bed
    Screened from the public gaze.

The horse-brass shines, the kettle sings,
    The cup of China tea
Is tasted among cared-for things
    Ranged round for me to see –

Lincoln, by Valentine & Co.,
    Now yellowish brown and stained,
But there some fifty years ago
    Her Harry was ordained;

Outside the Church at Woodhall Spa
    The smiling groom and bride,
And here's his old tobacco jar
    Dried lavender inside.

I do not like to ask if he
    Was "High" or "Low" or "Broad"
Lest such a question seem to be
    A mockery of our Lord.

Her full grey eyes look far beyond
    The little room and me
To village church and village pond
    And ample rectory.

She sees her children each in place
    Eyes downcast as they wait,
She hears her Harry murmur Grace
    Then heaps the porridge plate.

Aroused at seven, to bed by ten,
    They fully lived each day,
Dead sons, so motor-bike-mad then,
    And daughters far away.

Now when the bells for Eucharist
    Sound in the Market Square,
With sunshine struggling through the mist
    And Sunday in the air,

The veil between her and her dead
    Dissolves and shows them clear,
The Consecration Prayer is said
    And all of them are near.

JOHN BETJEMAN
A Few Late Chrysanthemums

When I'm Alone

"When I'm alone" – the words tripped off his tongue
As though to be alone were nothing strange.
"When I was young," he said; *"when I was young. . . ."*

> I thought of age, and loneliness, and change.
> I thought how strange we grow when we're alone,
> And how unlike the selves that meet, and talk,
> And blow the candles out, and say good-night.
> *Alone* . . . The word is life endured and known.
> It is the stillness where our spirits walk
> And all but inmost faith is overthrown.

SIEGFRIED SASSOON
Collected Poems

A Card Comes

A Card comes to tell you
you should report
to have your eyes tested.

But your eyes melted in the fire
and the only tears, which soon dried,
fell in the chapel.

Other things still come –
invoices, subscription renewals,
shiny plastic cards promising credit –
not much for a life spent
in the service of reality.

You need answer none of them.
Nor my asking you for one drop
of succour in my own hell.

Do not cry, I tell myself,
The whole thing is a comedy
and comedies end happily.

The fire will come out of the sun
And I shall look in the heart of it.

PETER PORTER
Non Piangere, Liù

Home Is So Sad

What I had now was a house too absurdly spacious for
me, a premises. It enclosed its irrelevant furniture, its
wardrobes and drawers containing clothes and miscellanea
whose former owner no longer needed them and yet
which I could not bring myself to part with or dispose of.
They variously rebuked or mocked me. Blouses,
collections of porcelain thimbles, half-finished knitting. I
could have been no more lonely in a chaos of rocks.

TED WALKER
The Last of England

Home is so sad. It stays as it was left,
Shaped to the comfort of the last to go
As if to win them back. Instead, bereft
Of anyone to please, it withers so,
Having no heart to put aside the theft

And turn again to what it started as,
A joyous shot at how things ought to be,
Long fallen wide. You can see how it was:
Look at the pictures and the cutlery.
The music in the piano stool. That vase.

PHILIP LARKIN
The Whitsun Weddings

When You Were Here

When you were here, ah foolish then!
I scarcely knew I loved you, dear.
I know it now, I know it when
You are no longer here.

When you were here, I sometimes tired,
Ah me! that you so loved me, dear.
Now, in these weary days desired,
You are no longer here.

When you were here, did either know
That each so loved the other, dear?
But that was long and long ago:
You are no longer here.

ARTHUR SYMONS
Silhouettes

Mary: It Is The Evening Hour

It is the evening hour,
    How silent all doth lie:
The hornèd moon she shows her face
    In the river with the sky.
Prest by the path on which we pass
The flaggy lake lies still as glass.

Spirit of her I love,
    Whispering to me
Stories of sweet visions as I rove,
    Here stop, and crop with me
Sweet flowers that in the still hour grew –
We'll take them home, nor shake off the bright dew.

Mary, or sweet spirit of thee,
    As the bright sun shines tomorrow,
Thy dark eyes these flowers shall see,
    Gathered by me in sorrow,
In the still hour when my mind was free
To walk alone – yet wish I walked with thee.

JOHN CLARE
Mary

Those That Are Gone

They shall not grow old, as we that are left grow old:
Age shall not weary them, nor the years condemn.
At the going down of the sun and in the morning
We will remember them.

LAURENCE BINYON
Poems for the Fallen

Solitude

When you have tidied all things for the night,
And while your thoughts are fading to their sleep,
You'll pause a moment in the late firelight,
Too sorrowful to weep.

The large and gentle furniture has stood
In sympathetic silence all the day
With that old kindness of domestic wood;
Nevertheless the haunted room will say:
"Someone must be away."

The little dog rolls over half awake,
Stretches his paws, yawns, looking up at you,
Wags his tail very slightly for your sake,
That you may feel he is unhappy too.

A distant engine whistles, or the floor
Creaks, or the wandering night-wind bangs a door.

Silence is scattered like a broken glass.
The minutes prick their ears and run about,
Then one by one subside again and pass
Sedately in, monotonously out.

You bend your head and wipe away a tear.
Solitude walks one heavy step more near.

HAROLD MONRO
Solitude

Might-Have-Been

Look in my face; my name is Might-have-been;
     I am also called No-more, Too-late, Farewell;
      Unto thine ear I hold the dead-sea shell
Cast up thy Life's foam-fretted feet between;
Unto thine eyes the glass where that is seen
      Which had Life's form and Love's, but by my spell
      Is now a shaken shadow intolerable,
Of ultimate things unuttered the frail screen.

Mark me, how still I am! But should there dart
      One moment through thy soul the soft surprise
      Of that winged Peace that lulls the breath of sighs –
Then shalt thou see me smile, and turn apart
Thy visage to mine ambush at thy heart
      Sleepless with cold commemorative eyes.

DANTE GABRIEL ROSSETTI
A Superscription

As Of Old

My dead love came to me, and said:
    "God gives me one hour's rest
To spend upon the earth with thee:
    How shall we spend it best?"

"Why, as of old," I said, and so
    We quarrelled as of old,
But when I turned to make my peace
    That one short hour was told . . .

STEPHEN PHILLIPS
The Apparition

My Old Dutch

I calls 'er Sal.
'Er proper name is Sairer;
An' yer may find a gal
As you'd consider fairer
She ain't a angel – she can start
A jawin' till it makes yer smart;
She's just a woman, bless 'er 'eart,
Is my old gal. . . .

We've been together now for forty years,
An' it don't seem a day too much;
There ain't a lady livin' in the land
As I'd swop for my dear old Dutch.

I sees yer, Sal –
Yer pretty ribbons sportin':
Many years now, old gal,
Since them young days of courtin'.
I ain't a coward, still I trust
When we've to part, as part we must,
That Death may come and take me fust
To wait . . . my pal.

ALBERT CHEVALIER
My Old Dutch

Some We Loved

Lo! some we loved, the loveliest and the best
That Time and Fate of all their Vintage prest,
     Have drunk their Cup a Round or two before,
And one by one crept silently to Rest.

EDWARD FITZGERALD
Rubaiyat of Omar Khayyam

The Wife A-Lost

Since I noo mwore de zee your feace
        Up stears or down below,
I'll zit me in the lwonesome pleace.
        Where flat-bough'd beech do grow;
Below the beeches' bough, my love,
        Where you did never come,
And I don't look to meet ye now,
        As I do look at hwome.

Since you noo mwore be at my zide,
        In walks in zummer het,
I'll goo alwone where mist do ride,
        Drough trees a-drippen wet;
Below the rain-wet bough, my love,
        Where you did never come,
An' I don't grieve to miss ye now,
        As I do grieve at hwome.

Since now bezide my dinner-bwoard
        Your vaice do never sound
I'll eat the bit I can avword
        A-vield upon the ground;
Below the darksome bough, my love,
        Where you did never dine,
An' I don't grieve to miss ye now,
        As I at hwome do pine.

Since I do miss your vaice an' feace
    In prayer at eventide,
I'll pray wi oone sad vaice vor greace
    To goo where you do bide;
Above the tree an' bough, my love,
    Where you be gone avore,
An' be a-waiten vor me now,
    To come vor evermwore.

WILLIAM BARNES
The Wife A-Lost

Going Home

Long are the hours the sun is above,
But when evening comes I go home to my love.

I'm away the daylight hours and more,
Yet she comes not down to open the door.

She does not meet me upon the stair –
She sits in my chamber and waits for me there.

As I enter the room she does not move:
I always walk straight up to my love;

And she lets me take my wonted place
At her side, and gaze in her dear, dear face.

There as I sit, from her head thrown back
Her hair falls straight in a shadow black

Aching and hot as my tired eyes be,
She is all that I wish to see.

And in my weary and toil-dinned ear,
She says all the things that I wish to hear.

Duskier and duskier grows the room,
Yet I see her best in the darker gloom.

When the winter eves are early and cold,
The firelight hours are a dream of gold.

And so I sit here night by night,
In rest and enjoyment of love's delight.

But a knock at the door, a step on the stair
Will startle, alas, my love from her chair.

If a stranger comes she will not stay:
At the first alarm she is off and away.

And he wonders, my guest, usurping her throne,
That I sit so much by myself alone.

ROBERT BRIDGES

Remembrance of Things Past

Voices

Ideal and dearly beloved voices
of those who are dead, or of those
who are lost to us like the dead.

Sometimes they speak to us in our dreams;
sometimes in thought the mind hears them.

And for a moment with their echo other echoes
return from the first poetry of our lives –
like music that extinguishes the far-off night.

C. P. CAVAFY
Complete Poems
translated by Rae Dalven

A Memory of His Mother

I do not think of you lying in the wet clay
Of a Monaghan graveyard: I see
You walking down a lane among the poplars
On your way to the station, or happily
Going to a second Mass on a summer Sunday –
You meet me and you say:
"Don't forget to see about the cattle –"
Among your earthiest words the angels stray.

And I think of you walking along a headland
Of green oats in June
So full of repose, so rich with life –
And I see us meeting at the end of a town
On a fair day by accident, after
The bargains are all made and we can walk
Together through the shops and stalls and markets
Free in the oriental streets of thought.

O you are not lying in the wet clay,
For it is harvest evening now and we
Are piling up the ricks against the moonlight
And you smile up at us – eternally.

PATRICK KAVANAGH
A Memory of his Mother

A Memory of His Father

Only last week, walking the hushed fields
Of our most lovely Meath, now thinned by November,
I came to where the road from Laracor leads
To the Boyne river – that seemed more lake than river,
Stretched in uneasy light and stript of reeds.

And walking alongside an old weir
Of my people's, where nothing stirs – only the shadowed
Leaden flight of a heron up the lead air –
I went unmanly with grief, knowing how my father,
Happy though captive in years, walked last with me there.

Yes, happy in Meath with me for a day
He walked, taking stock of herds hid in their own breathing;
And naming colts, gusty as wind, once steered by his hand;
Lightnings winked in the eyes that were half shy in greeting
Old friends – the wild blades, when he gallivanted the land.

For that proud, wayward man now my heart breaks –
Breaks for that man whose mind was a secret eyrie,
Whose kind hand was sole signet of his race,
Who curbed me, scorned my green ways, yet increasingly loved me
Till Death drew its grey blind down his face.

And yet I am pleased that even my reckless ways
Are living shades of his rich calms and passions –
Witnesses for him and for those faint namesakes
With whom now he is one, under yew branches,
Yes, one in a graven silence no bird speaks.

F. R. HIGGINS
Father and Son

The Light of Other Days

Oft, in the stilly night,
    Ere Slumber's chain has bound me,
Fond Memory brings the light
    Of other days around me;
        The smiles, the tears,
        Of boyhood's years,
    The words of love then spoken;
        The eyes that shone,
        Now dimm'd and gone,
    The cheerful hearts now broken!
Thus, in the stilly night,
    Ere Slumber's chain has bound me,
Sad Memory brings the light
    Of other days around me.

When I remember all
    The friends, so linked together,
I've seen them round me fall,
    Like leaves in wintry weather;
        I feel like one,
        Who treads alone
    Some banquet-hall deserted,
        Whose lights are fled,
        Whose garlands dead,
    And all but he departed.
Thus, in the stilly night,

Ere Slumber's chain has bound me,
Sad Memory brings the light
      Of other days around me.

National Airs

John Anderson My Jo

John Anderson my jo, John
      When we were first acquent,
Your locks were like the raven,
      Your bonny brow was brent;
But now your brow is beld, John,
      Your locks are like the snaw;
But blessings on your frosty pow,
      John Anderson my jo.

John Anderson my jo, John
      We clamb the hill the gither;
And mony a canty day, John
      We've had wi' ane anither;
Now we maun totter down, John,
      And hand in hand we'll go;
And sleep the gither at the foot,
      John Anderson my jo.

ROBERT BURNS

Remember Me

Remember me when I am gone away,
      Gone far away into the silent land;
      When you can no more hold me by the hand
Nor I half turn to go, yet turning stay.
Remember me when no more day by day
      You tell me of our future that you planned:
      Only remember me; you understand
It will be late to counsel then or pray.
Yet if you should forget me for a while
      And afterwards remember, do not grieve:
      For if the darkness and corruption leave
      A vestige of the thoughts that once I had,
Better by far you should forget and smile
      Than that you should remember and be sad.

CHRISTINA ROSSETTI
Goblin Market and Other Poems

Two and Thirty Years Ago

All along the valley, stream that flashest white,
Deepening thy voice with the deepening of the night
All along the valley, where thy waters flow,
I walk'd with one I loved two and thirty years ago.
All along the valley while I walk'd to-day,
The two and thirty years were a mist that rolls away;
For all along the valley, down thy rocky bed
Thy living voice to me was as the voice of the dead,
And all along the valley, by rock and cave and tree,
The voice of the dead was a living voice to me.

ALFRED, LORD TENNYSON
In the Valley of Cauteretz

Spring

When lilacs last in the dooryard bloom'd
And the great star early droop'd in the western sky in the night,
I mourn'd, and yet shall mourn with ever-returning spring.

Ever-returning spring, trinity sure to me you bring,
Lilac blooming perennial and drooping star in the west,
And thought of him I love.

WALT WHITMAN
Memories of President Lincoln

Summer

A dozen sparrows scuttled on the frost.
We watched them play. We stood at the window,
And, if you saw us, then you saw a ghost
In duplicate. I tied her nightgown's bow.
She watched and recognized the passers-by.
Had they looked up, they'd know that she was ill –
"Please, do not draw the curtains when I die" –
From all the flowers on the windowsill.

"It's such a shame," she said. "Too ill, too quick."
"I would have liked us to have gone away."
We closed our eyes together, dreaming France,
Its meadows, rivers, woods and *jouissance*.
I counted summers, our love's arithmetic.
"Some other day, my love, Some other day."

DOUGLAS DUNN
Elegies

Autumn

Now sits the autumn cricket in the grass,
And on the gravel crawls the chilly bee;
Near to its close and none too soon for me
Draws the dull year, in which has come to pass
The changing of the happy child I was
Into this quiet creature people see
Stitching a seam with careful industry
To deaden you, who died on Michaelmas.
Ages ago the purple aconite
Laid its dark hoods about it on the ground,
And roses budded small and were content;
Swallows are south long since and out of sight;
With you the phlox and asters also went;
Nor can my laughter anywhere be found.

EDNA ST VINCENT MILLAY
from Mine the Harvest

Winter

The night is freezing fast,
    To-morrow comes December
        And winterfalls of old
Are with me from the past;
    And chiefly I remember
        How Dick would hate the cold.

Fall, winter, fall; for he,
    Prompt hand and headpiece clever,
        Has woven a winter robe,
And made of earth and sea
    His overcoat for ever,
        And wears the turning globe.

A. E. HOUSMAN
Last Poems

Echo

At the mid hour of night, when stars are weeping, I fly
To the lone vale we loved when life was warm in thine eye
   And I think that if spirits can steal from the regions of air
    To revisit past scenes of delight, thou wilt come to me there
And tell me our love is remembered, even in the sky!

Then I sing the wild song it once was rapture to hear
When our voices, commingling, breathed like one on the ear
   And as Echo far off through the vale my sad orison rolls,
    I think, oh, my love! 'tis thy voice from the kingdom of souls
Faintly answering still the notes once that were so dear.

THOMAS MOORE
Irish Melodies

That Tune

A foolish rhythm turns in my idle head
As a wind-mill turns in the wind on an empty sky.
Why is it when love, which men call deathless, is dead,
That memory, men call fugitive, will not die?
Is love not dead? yet I hear that tune if I lie
Dreaming awake in the night on my lonely bed,
And an old thought turns with the old tune in my head
As a wind-mill turns in the wind on an empty sky.

ARTHUR SYMONS
Images of Good and Evil

On Wakening

Why did I dream of you last night?
Now morning is pushing back hair with grey light
Memories strike home, like slaps in the face:
Raised on elbow, I stare at the pale fog
beyond the window.

So many things I had thought forgotten
Return to my mind with stranger pain:
–Like letters that arrive addressed to someone
Who left the house so many years ago.

PHILIP LARKIN
Collected Poems

Whispers

As birds are fitted to the boughs
That blossom on the tree
And whisper when the south wind blows
So was my love to me.

And still she blossoms in my mind
And whispers softly, though
The clouds are fitted to the wind
The wind is to the snow.

LOUIS SIMPSON
Selected Poems

The Widow

Grief now hath pacified her face;
Even hope might share so still a place.
Yet, if – in silence of her heart –
A memoried voice or footstep start,
Or a chance word of ecstasy
Cry through dim-cloistered memory,
Into her eyes her soul will steal
To gaze on the irrevocable –
As if death had not power to keep
One, who had loved her long, so long asleep . . .

WALTER DE LA MARE
Collected Poems

There Was a Time

There was a time when meadow, grove and stream,
The earth, and every common sight
      To me did seem
    Apparelled in celestial light.
The glory and the freshness of a dream.
It is not now as it hath been of yore –
    Turn whereso'er I may.
      By night or day,
The things which I have seen I now can see now more.

    The Rainbow comes and goes,
    And lovely is the Rose;
    The Moon doth with delight
Look round her when the heavens are bare;
    Waters on a starry night
    Are beautiful and fair;
    The sunshine is a glorious birth;
    But yet I know, where'er I go
That there has passed away a glory from the earth.

WILLIAM WORDSWORTH
Intimations of Immortality

The Happiest Pair

We were the happiest pair of human kind:
The rolling year its various course performed,
And back returned again;
Another and another smiling came,
And saw our happiness unchanged remain,
Still in her golden chain
Harmonious concord did our wishes bind:
Our studies, pleasures, taste the same.
O fatal, fatal stroke!
That all this pleasing fabric love had raised
Of rare felicity,
On which ev'n wanton vice with envy gazed,
And every scheme of bliss our heart had formed
With soothing hope for many a future day,
In one sad moment broke!

GEORGE LYTTELTON, LORD LYTTELTON
Monody on the Death of his Lady

Joys Once Shared

There is no greater pain than to recall a time of happiness
in one of sorrow.

DANTE ALIGHIERI
Divine Comedy, Inferno, v.121

Oh doe not die, says Donne, *for I shall hate*
All women so. How false the sentence rings.
Women? But in a life made desolate
It is the joys once shared that have the stings.

To take the old walks alone, or not at all,
To order one pint where I ordered two,
To think of, and then not to make, the small
Time-honoured joke (senseless to all but you);

To laugh (oh, one'll laugh), to talk upon
Themes that we talked upon when you were there,
To make some poor pretence of going on,
Be kind to one's old friends, and seem to care,

While no one (O God) through the years will say
The simplest, common word in just your way.

C. S. LEWIS
Poems

The Land of Lost Content

Into my heart an air that kills
    From yon far country blows:
What are those blue remembered hills,
    What spires, what farms are those?

That is the land of lost content,
    I see it shining plain,
The happy highways where I went
    And cannot come again.

A. E. HOUSMAN
A Shropshire Lad

De Profundis

Abide With Me

Abide with me; fast falls the eventide;
    The darkness deepens; Lord, with me abide;
When other helpers fail, and comforts flee,
    Help of the helpless, O, abide with me.

HENRY FRANCIS LYTE
Abide with Me

Grief's Circle

Tonight all the hells of young grief have opened again; the mad words, the bitter resentment, the fluttering in the stomach, the nightmare unreality, the wallowed-in tears. For in grief nothing "stays put". One keeps on emerging from a phase, but it always recurs. Round and round. Everything repeats. Am I going in circles, or dare I hope I am on a spiral?

But if a spiral, am I going up or down it?

How often – will it be for always? – how often will the vast emptiness astonish me like a complete novelty and make me say, "I never realized my loss till this moment"? The same leg is cut off time after time. The first plunge of the knife into the flesh is felt again and again.

They say "The coward dies many times"; so does the beloved. Didn't the eagle find a fresh liver to tear in Prometheus every time it dined?

C. S. LEWIS
A Grief Observed

He Is Not Here

Dark house, by which once more I stand
  Here in the long unlovely street
  Doors, where my heart was used to beat
So quickly, waiting for a hand,

A hand that can be clasped no more –
  Behold me, for I cannot sleep,
  And like a guilty thing I creep
At earliest morning to the door.

He is not here; but far away
  The noise of life begins again,
  And ghastly thro' the drizzling rain
On the bald street breaks the blank day.

ALFRED, LORD TENNYSON
In Memoriam

Empty Places

There are a hundred places where I fear
To go, – so with his memory they brim.
And entering with relief some quiet place
Where never fell his foot or shone his face
I say, "There is no memory of him here!"
And so stand stricken, so remembering him.

EDNA ST VINCENT MILLAY
Time does not bring relief

My heart was darkened over with grief, and whatever I
looked at was death. Where I lived was a torment to me;
even my own home filled me with sorrow. Those things
which my friend and I used to share together, now that I
was without him, tortured me like the lash of a whip. My
eyes looked for him everywhere and could not find him.
All places were hateful to me, because he was not there.
They could not say to me now, "Look he will soon
come", as they used to say when he was alive and away
from me. I had become a great enigma to myself and
asked my soul why it was so sad and why it caused me so
much distress. And my soul did not know what to answer.
If I said, "Trust in God," my soul very rightly did not
obey me, because the dearest friend whom it had lost was
more real and better than the fantastic god in whom it was
told to trust. Only tears were my consolation, and tears
had taken the place of my friend in my heart's love.

SAINT AUGUSTINE OF HIPPO
The Confessions

When Love Is Done

The night has a thousand eyes,
    And the day but one;
Yet the light of the bright world dies
    With the dying sun.

The mind has a thousand eyes,
    And the heart but one;
Yet the light of a whole life dies
    When love is done.

FRANCIS WILLIAM BOURDILLON
Light

Half Of Me

I used to wonder that other men and women were alive when death had come to my friend, whom I had loved as though he would never die. Even more I wondered that I, who was his other self, was still alive when he was dead. Someone once spoke of his friend as "the half of my own soul". I agree, for I felt that my soul and that of my friend had been one soul in two bodies. So I had a horror of going on living, because I did not wish to live on as a half-person. And perhaps, too, that was the reason why I was afraid to die – lest he, whom I had loved so much, should die completely.

SAINT AUGUSTINE OF HIPPO
The Confessions

My body's self deserts me now,
    The half of me that was her own,
Since all I knew of brightness died
    Half of me lingers, half is gone.

The face that was like hawthorn bloom
    Was my right foot and my right side;
And my right foot and my right eye
    Were no more mine than hers who died.

——————————————————————— *De Profundis*

Poor is the share of me that's left
    Since half of me died with my wife
I shudder at the words I speak;
    Dear God, that girl was half my life. . . .

MUIREADACH O'DALAIGH
translated by Frank O'Connor

Too Soon

The fairest things have fleetest end,
    Their scent survives their close:
But the rose's scent is bitterness
    To him that loved the rose . . .

FRANCIS THOMPSON
Daisy

Too soon, too soon comes Death to show
We love more deeply than we know.
The rain, that fell upon the height
Too gently to be called delight,
Within the dark vale reappears
As a wild cataract of tears;
And love in life should strive to see
Sometimes what love in death would be.

COVENTRY PATMORE
The Victories of Love

Life's Chequer-Board

'Tis all a Chequer-board of Nights and Days
Where Destiny with Men for Pieces plays:
    Hither and thither moves, and mates, and slays,
And one by one back in the Closet lays.

EDWARD FITZGERALD
Rubaiyat of Omar Khayyam

De Profundis

Pure Death

We looked, we loved, and therewith instantly
Death became terrible to you and me.
By love we disenthralled our natural terror
From every comfortable philosopher
Or tall, grey doctor of divinity:
Death stood at last in his true rank and order.

It happened soon, so wild of heart were we,
Exchange of gifts grew to a malady:
Their worth rose always higher on each side
Till there seemed nothing but ungivable pride
That yet remained ungiven, and this degree
Called a conclusion not to be denied.

Then we at least bethought ourselves, made shift
And simultaneously this final gift
Gave: each with shaking hand unlocks
The sinister, long, brass-bound coffin-box,
Unwraps pure death, with such bewilderment
As greeted our love's first acknowledgement.

ROBERT GRAVES
Collected Poems

Hail and Farewell

By ways remote and distant waters sped
Brother, to thy sad grave-side am I come,
That I may give the last gifts to the dead,
And vainly parley with thine ashes dumb,
Since she who now bestows and now denies
Hath ta'en thee, hapless brother, from mine eyes.

But lo! these gifts, the heirlooms of past years,
Are made sad things to grace thy coffin shell,
Take them, all drenchèd with a brother's tears,
And, brother, for all time, hail and farewell.

CATULLUS
Carmen 101
translated by Aubrey Beardsley

Surprised By Joy

Surprised by joy – impatient as the wind
  I turned to share the transport – O! with whom
  But Thee, deep buried in the silent tomb,
That spot which no vicissitude can find?
Love, faithful love, recalled thee to my mind –
  But how could I forget thee? Through what power,
  Even for the least division of an hour,
Have I been so beguiled as to be blind
To my most grievous loss! That thought's return
  Was the worst pang that sorrow ever bore,
Save one, one only, when I stood forlorn,
  Knowing my heart's best treasure was no more;
That neither present time, nor years unborn
  Could to my sight that heavenly face restore.

WILLIAM WORDSWORTH
Poems 1815

By Day By Night

How can I, then, return in happy plight,
That am debarr'd the benefit of rest?
When day's oppression is not eas'd by night,
By day by night, and night by day, oppress'd?
And each, though enemies to eithers' reign,
Do in consent shake hands to torture me;
The one by toil, the other to complain
How far I toil, still farther off from thee.
I tell the day, to please him thou art bright,
And dost him grace when clouds do blot the heaven:
So flatter I the swart-complexion'd night,
When sparkling stars twire not thou gild'st the even.
    But day doth daily draw my sorrows longer,
    And night doth nightly make grief's strength
        seem stronger.

WILLIAM SHAKESPEARE
Sonnets 28

My Days Go On

But as soon as the pressure of work or people eases off,
back rushes the tidal wave of longing and loneliness and
pain, almost unchanged since the very first. I stand like a
sombre black rock while it washes and swirls over me,
unable to do anything but just endure and wait. This is
what happened this morning, and I was full of wonder at
the self-deception which had made me seem (as I suppose)
to others to be making a go of my life. This morning I felt
myself drowning in envy for everyone who had someone
to be responsible for, to be responsible for them, to discuss
their worries and minute daily experiences with; to go and
lean on in moments of weakness, huddle up to for blessed
animal warmth, to love and be loved by. Oh, what endless
courage one has to keep stoking up to walk one's cold
frightening path alone!

FRANCES PARTRIDGE
Hanging On

The face which, duly as the sun,
Rose up for me with life begun,
To mark all bright hours of the day
With homely love, is dimmed away –
And yet my days go on, go on.

The tongue which, like a stream, could run
Smooth music from the roughest stone,
And every morning with "Good day"
Make each day good, is hushed away –
And yet my days go on, go on.

The heart which, like a staff, was one
For mine to lean and rest upon,
The strongest on the longest day
With steadfast love, is caught away –
And yet my days go on, go on . . .

ELIZABETH BARRETT BROWNING
De Profundis

Search

Passive, your glove allows me to enter
its five black-soft tunnels
the tips however remain uninhabited,
your fingers having been longer than mine.

The words you typed and left, expecting to return,
file out across their electronic lawn.
I caress them with the cursor, like a medium
stroking the table at a seance.

At your pain on the answerphone tape my voice
sticks, as at the gaps in a linguaphone lesson.
In tears, I sort the wafers of your clothes for friends –
straitjacketed in card you watch, and seem unmoved.

At last, day buckles and, awake in bed, I find you:
the deadweight limbs we turned two-hourly
and powdered to protect your baffled skin
become my own, crook'd flat along the sheet

and from the soft lame triangle that your mouth became
you breathe your childhood out upon my pillow.
Wearing the features of our father,
your frightened face sleeps inside mine.

JANE DRAYCOTT
Braving the Dark (in memory of her brother)

The Kaleidoscope

To climb these stairs again, bearing a tray,
Might be to find you pillowed with your books,
Your inventories listing gowns and frocks
As if preparing for a holiday.
Or, turning from the landing, I might find
My presence watched through your kaleidoscope,
A symmetry of husbands, each redesigned
In lovely forms of foresight, prayer and hope.
I climb these stairs a dozen times a day
And, by that open door, wait, looking in
At where you died. My hands become a tray
Offering me, my flesh, my soul, my skin.
Grief wrongs us so. I stand, and wait, and cry
For the absurd forgiveness, not knowing why.

DOUGLAS DUNN
Elegies

If Only . . .

O that 'twere possible
After long grief and pain
To find the arms of my true love
Round me once again! . . .

A shadow flits before me,
Not thou, but like to thee:
Ah Christ, that it were possible
For one short hour to see
The souls we loved, that they might tell us
What and where they be!

ALFRED, LORD TENNYSON
Maud

A Dream

Methought I saw my late espousèd saint
    Brought to me like Alcestis from the grave,
    Whom Jove's great son to her glad husband gave,
    Rescued from death by force though pale and faint.
Mine as whom washed from spot of childbed taint,
    Purification in the old Law did save,
    And such, as yet once more I trust to have
    Full sight of her in Heaven without restraint,
Came vested all in white, pure as her mind;
    Her face was veiled, yet to my fancied sight,
    Love, sweetness, goodness, in her person shined
So clear, as in no face with more delight.
    But O as to embrace me she inclined
    I waked, she fled, and day brought back my night.

JOHN MILTON

The Wind

As day did darken on the dewless grass
There still wi' nwone a-come by me,
To stay a-while at hwome by me;
Within the house, all dumb by me,
I zot me sad as the eventide did pass.

An' there a win'-blast shook the rattlen door,
An' seemed, as win' did mwone without,
As if my Jeane, alwone without,
A-stannen on the stone without,
Were there a-come wi' happiness oonce more.

I went to door; an' out vrom trees above
My head, upon the blast by me,
Sweet blossoms wer a-cast by me,
As if my love, a-past by me,
Did fling em down – a token ov her love.

"Sweet blossoms o' the tree where I do murn,"
I thought, "if you did blow vor her,
Vor apples that should grow vor her,
A-vallen down below vor her,
O then how happy I should zee you kern."

But no. Too soon I voun' my charm abroke.
Noo comely soul in white like her –
Noo soul a-steppen light like her –
An' nwone o' comely height like her –
Went by; but all my grief agean awoke.

WILLIAM BARNES

An Empty Heart

"You know poor Mr. Dodsley has lost his wife; I believe
he is much affected. I hope he will not suffer so much as I
yet suffer for the loss of mine. . . . I have ever since
seemed to myself broken off from mankind; a kind of
solitary wanderer in the wild of life, without any direction,
or fixed point of view: a gloomy gazer on a world to
which I have little relation."

SAMUEL JOHNSON
Boswell's Life of Johnson

Age, and the deaths, and the ghosts.
Her having gone away
in spirit from me. Hosts
of regrets come & find me empty.

I don't feel this will change.
I don't want any thing
or person, familiar or strange.
I don't think I will sing

any more just now,
or ever. I must start
to sit with a blind brow
above an empty heart.

JOHN BERRYMAN
He Resigns

What Answer Can I Give?

King Philip: You are as fond of grief as of your child.

Constance: Grief fills the room up of my absent child,
Lies in his bed, walks up and down with me,
Puts on his pretty looks, repeats his words,
Remembers me of all his gracious parts,
Stuffs out his vacant garments with his form;
Then have I reason to be fond of grief.

WILLIAM SHAKESPEARE
King John, III.4.

She Was Mine

"Thy tears o'erprize thy loss! Thy wife
In what was she particular?
Others of comely face and life,
Others as chaste and warm there are,
And when they speak they seem to sing;
Beyond her sex she was not wise;
And there is no more common thing
Than kindness in a woman's eyes.
Then wherefore weep so long and fast,
Why so exceedingly repine?
Say, how has thy Beloved surpassed
So much all others?" – "She was mine."

COVENTRY PATMORE
The Espousals

Silent Grief

I tell you, hopeless grief is passionless
That only men incredulous of despair,
Half-taught in anguish, through the midnight air
Beat upwards to God's throne in loud access
Of shrieking and reproach. Full desertness
In souls, as countries, lieth silent-bare
Under the blanching, vertical eye-glare
Of the absolute Heavens. Deep-hearted man, express
Grief for thy Dead in silence like to death –
Most like a monumental statue set
In everlasting watch and moveless woe,
Till itself crumble to the dust beneath.
Touch it: the marble eyelids are not wet;
If it could weep, it could arise and go.

ELIZABETH BARRETT BROWNING
Grief

If Grief Could Burn Out

The worst thing about grief is the length of time during which the experience lasts. For the first weeks one is in a state of shock. But the agony lasts long after the state of shock comes to an end. After a year, or about two, the agony gives way to a dull ache, a sort of void. During the night in one's dreams, and in the morning when one wakes, one is vaguely aware that something is wrong and, when waking is complete, one knows exactly what it is.

LORD HAILSHAM OF ST MARYLEBONE
A Sparrow's Flight

If grief could burn out
Like a sunken coal,
The heart would rest quiet,
The unrent soul
Be still as a veil;
But I have watched all night

The fire grow silent,
The grey ash soft:
And I stir the stubborn flint
The flames have left,
And grief stirs, and the deft
Heart lies impotent.

PHILIP LARKIN
The North Ship

Do This Favour For Me

Dear gentle soul, who went so soon away
Departing from this life in discontent,
Repose in that far sky to which you went
While on this earth I linger in dismay.
In the ethereal seat where you must be,
If you consent to memories of our sphere,
Recall the love which, burning pure and clear,
So often in my eyes you used to see!
If then, in the incurable, long anguish
Of having lost you, as I pine and languish,
You see some merit – do this favour for me
And to the God who cut your life short, pray
That he as early to your sight restore me
As from my own he swept you far away.

LUIS DE CAMOENS
Translated by Roy Campbell

My Dearest Dust

My dearest dust, could not thy hasty day
Afford thy drowszy patience leave to stay
One hower longer: so that we might either
Sate up, or gone to bedd together?
But since thy finisht labour hath possest
Thy weary limbs with early rest,
Enjoy it sweetly: and thy widdowe bride
Shall soone repose her by thy slumbring side.
Whose business, now, is only to prepare
My nightly dress, and call to prayre:
Mine eyes wax heavy and ye day growes old.
The dew falls thick, my belovd growes cold.
Draw, draw ye closed curtaynes: and make roome:
My deare, my dearest dust; I come, I come.

LADY CATHERINE DYER
Epitaph on the Monument of Sir William Dyer
at Colmworth, Bedfordshire

Not Unto Us

Not unto us, O Lord,
Not unto us the rapture of the day,
The peace of night, or love's divine surprise,
High heart, high speech, high deeds 'mid honouring eyes;
For at thy word
All these are taken away.

Not unto us, O Lord:
To us thou givest the scorn, the scourge, the scar,
The ache of life, the loneliness of death,
The insufferable sufficiency of breath;
And with Thy sword
Thou piercest very far.

Not unto us, O Lord:
Nay, Lord, but unto her be all things given –
May light and life and earth and sky be blasted –
But let not all that wealth of loss be wasted:
Let Hell afford
The pavement of her Heaven!

HENRY CUST
Non Nobis, Domine

Love endures

Our Love Hath No Decay

All other things, to their destruction draw,
Only our love hath no decay;
This, no to-morrow hath, nor yesterday,
Running it never runs from us away,
But truly keeps his first, last, everlasting day.

JOHN DONNE
The Anniversary

How Do I Love Thee?

How do I love thee? Let me count the ways.
I love to the depth and breadth and height
My soul can reach, when feeling out of sight
For the ends of Being and ideal Grace.
I love thee to the level of every day's
Most quiet need, by sun and candle light.
I love thee freely, as men strive for Right;
I love thee purely, as they turn from Praise.
I love thee with the passion put to use
In my old griefs, and with my childhood's faith.
I love thee with a love I seemed to lose
With my lost saints – I love thee with the breath,
Smiles, tears, of all my life! and if God choose,
I shall but love thee better after death.

ELIZABETH BARRETT BROWNING
Sonnets from the Portuguese

My True Love Hath My Heart

It is often said that something may survive of a person after his death, if that person was an artist and put a little of himself into his work. It is perhaps in the same way that a sort of cutting taken from one person and grafted onto the heart of another continues to carry on its existence even when the person from whom it had been detached has perished.

MARCEL PROUST
Remembrance of Things Past
translated by C. K. Scott Moncrieff

My true love hath my heart, and I have his,
By just exchange, one for the other given.
I hold his dear, and mine he cannot miss:
There never was a better bargain driven.
     My true love hath my heart, and I have his.

His heart in me, keeps me and him in one,
My heart in him, his thoughts and senses guides:
He loves my heart, for once it was his own:
I cherish his, because in me it bides . . .
My true love hath my heart, and I have his.

SIR PHILIP SIDNEY
The Countess of Pembroke's Arcadia

The Wedding Ring

The ring so worn, as you behold,
So thin, so pale, is yet of gold:
The passion such it was to prove;
Worn with life's care, love yet was love.

GEORGE CRABBE
Poetical Works

Love Indestructible

But true Love is a durable fire
    In the mind ever burning;
Never sick, never old, never dead,
    From itself never turning.

SIR WALTER RALEGH
As you came from the Holy Land

They sin who tell us Love can die.
    With life all other passions fly,
        All others are but vanity.
    In Heaven Ambition cannot dwell,
    Nor Avarice in the vaults of Hell;
    Earthly those passions of the Earth,
They perish where they had their birth;
        But Love is indestructible.
    Its holy flame forever burneth,
From Heaven it came, to Heaven returneth;
    Too oft on Earth a troubled guest,
    At times deceived, at times opprest,
        It here is tried and purified,
    Then hath in Heaven its perfect rest:
    It soweth here with toil and care,
But the harvest time of Love is there.

ROBERT SOUTHEY
The Curse of Kehama

A Red, Red Rose

O my Luve's like a red, red rose
    That's newly sprung in June:
O my Luve's like the melodie
    That's sweetly play'd in tune—

As fair art thou, my bonie lass,
    So deep in luve am I:
And I will luve thee still, my Dear,
    Till a' the seas gang dry—

Till a' the seas gang dry, my Dear,
    And the rocks melt wi' the sun;
I will luve thee still, my Dear,
    While the sands o'life shall run—

And fare thee weel, my only Luve!
    And fare thee weel a while!
And I will come again, my Luve,
    Tho' it were ten thousand mile!

ROBERT BURNS
A Selection of Scots Songs

Nunc Dimittis

I am dying; but what of that?
Your hands are under my head,
And your tears are on my cheek
And I am happy at last –
Bitter has been the pain!
Yea I have paid the price
For this last moment with you
But all is well at the end;
Your hands are under my head,
And your tears are on my cheek.
So you love me, after all!
And I bless the eternal dark
Into which I sink and fall
That I've found you – at the last.

JOHN COWPER POWYS
Mandragora

No Need

I see an empty place at the table.
Whose? Who else's? Who am I kidding?
The boat's waiting. No need for oars
or a wind. I've left the key
in the same place. You know where.
Remember me and all we did together.
Now, hold me tight. That's it. Kiss me
hard on the lips. There. Now
let me go, my dearest. Let me go.
We shall not meet again in this life,
So kiss me goodbye now. Here, kiss me again.
Once more. There. That's enough.
Now, my dearest, let me go.
It's time to be on the way.

RAYMOND CARVER
A New Path to the Waterfall

Music When Soft Voices Die

Music, when soft voices die,
Vibrates in the memory –
Odours, when sweet violets sicken,
Live within the sense they quicken.

Rose-leaves, when the rose is dead,
Are heaped for the beloved's bed;
And so thy thoughts, when thou art gone,
Love itself shall slumber on.

PERCY BYSSHE SHELLEY
Posthumous Poems

Love Lies Here

Where is my love –
In silence and shadow she lies,
Under the April-grey calm waste of the skies;
And a bird above,
In the darkness tender and clear,
Keeps saying over and over, Love lies here!

Not that she's dead;
Only her soul is flown
Out of its last pure earthly mansion;
And cries instead
In the darkness, tender and clear,
Like the voice of a bird in the leaves, Love –
Love lies here!

WALTER DE LA MARE
Collected Poems

Come To Me

Come to me in the silence of the night;
    Come in the speaking silence of a dream;
Come with soft rounded cheeks and eyes as bright
    As sunlight on a stream;
        Come back in tears,
O memory, hope, love of finished years.

O dream how sweet, too sweet, too bitter sweet,
    Whose wakening should have been in Paradise,
Where souls brimful of love abide and meet;
    Where thirsting longing eyes
        Watch the slow door
That opening, letting in, lets out no more.

Yet come to me in dreams, that I may live
    My very life again though cold in death:
Come back to me in dreams, that I may give
    Pulse for pulse, breath for breath:
        Speak low, lean low.
As long ago, my love, how long ago!

CHRISTINA ROSSETTI
Goblin Market and Other Poems

Thee Shall I Hold

I, through all chances that are given to mortals,
    And through all fates that be,
So long as this close prison shall contain me,
    Yea, though a world shall sunder me and thee.

Thee shall I hold, in every fibre woven,
    Not with dumb lips, nor with averted face
Shall I behold thee, in my mind embrace thee,
    Instant and present, thou, in every place.

Yea, when the prison of this flesh is broken,
    And from the earth I shall have gone my way,
Whereso'er in the wide universe I stay me,
    There shall I bear thee, as I do to-day.

Think not the end, that from my body frees me,
    Breaks and unshackles from my love to thee;
Triumphs the soul above its house in ruin,
    Deathless, begot in immortality.

Still must she keep her senses and affections,
    Hold them as dear as life itself to be.
Could she choose death, then might she choose forgetting:
    Living, remembering, to eternity.

PAULINUS OF NOLA
To Ausonius
translated by Helen Waddell

Tears and Joys

If all the tears thou madest mine
Set in thy heaven for stars could shine,
> Thou shouldst not want for light,
> Even in the darkest night.

If all the joys thou madest one
To light my heart could be thy sun,
> So great would be the light
> Thou never shouldst have night.

MARGARET WOODS

The Strength Of Love

Set me as a seal upon thine heart, as a seal upon thine
arm: for love is strong as death: jealousy is cruel as the
grave: the coals thereof are coals of fire, which hath a most
vehement flame.

Many waters cannot quench love, neither can the
floods drown it: if a man would give all the substance of
his house for love, it would utterly be contemned.

THE SONG OF SOLOMON, 8.6–7
Lesson of the Mass of the Feast of St Mary Magdalene

Let me not to the marriage of true minds
Admit impediments. Love is not love
Which alters when it alteration finds,
Or bends with the remover to remove:
O, no! it is an ever-fixed mark,
That looks on tempests, and is never shaken;
It is the star to ever wandering bark,
Whose worth's unknown, although his height be taken.
Love's not Time's fool, though rosy lips and cheeks
Within his bending sickle's compass come;
Love alters not with his brief hours and weeks,
But bears it out even to the edge of doom.
    If this be error, and upon me proved,
    I never writ, nor no man ever loved.

WILLIAM SHAKESPEARE
Sonnets 115

Love endures ——————————————————— *95*

Not Death, But Love

I thought once how Theocritus had sung
Of the sweet years, the dear and wished-for years,
Who each one in a gracious hand appears
To bear a gift for mortals, old or young:
And, as I mused it in his antique tongue,
I saw, in gradual vision through my tears,
The sweet, sad years, the melancholy years,
Those of my own life, who by turns had flung
A shadow across me. Straightway I was 'ware,
So weeping, how a mystic Shape did move
Behind me, and drew me backward by the hair;
And a voice said in mastery while I strove . . .
"Guess now who holds thee?" "Death", I said. But, there,
The silver answer rang . . . "Not Death, but Love."

ELIZABETH BARRETT BROWNING
Sonnets from the Portuguese

To A Friend

If in the silent grave the dead
Ever find joy or solace in our grief –
The ache of love remembered, now a fallen leaf,
The tears for friendships long since sped –
Then, Calvus, be assured your wife
Feels not so much her sorrow for so short a life
As happiness in your love.

CATULLUS
Carmen 96

Love's Kingdom

Love is and was my Lord and King,
    And in his presence I attend
    To hear the tidings of my friend,
Which every hour his couriers bring.
Love is and was my King and Lord,
    And will be, tho' as yet I keep
    Within his court on earth, and sleep
Encompass'd by his faithful guard,
And hear at times a sentinel
    Who moves about from place to place,
    And whispers to the worlds of space,
In the deep night that all is well.

ALFRED, LORD TENNYSON
In Memoriam

While Over There

Seventeen years ago you said
    Something that sounded like Goodbye;
    And everybody thinks that your are dead,
      But I.

So I, as I grow stiff and cold
    To this and that say Goodbye too;
    And everybody sees that I am old
      But you.

    And one fine morning in a sunny lane
Some boy and girl will meet and kiss and swear
    That nobody can love their way again,
      While over there
You will have smiled, I shall have tossed your hair.

CHARLOTTE MEW

All Souls' Night

My love came back to me
Under the November tree
Shelterless and dim.
He put his hand upon my shoulder,
He did not think me strange or older,
Nor I, him.

FRANCES CORNFORD
Collected Poems

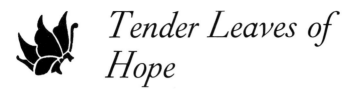

Tender Leaves of Hope

Grieve Not

What though the radiance which was once so bright
Be now for ever taken from my sight,
    Though nothing can bring back the hour
Of splendour in the grass, of glory in the flower;
    We will grieve not, rather find
    Strength in what remains behind;
    In the primal sympathy
    Which having been must ever be;
    In the soothing thoughts that spring
    Out of human suffering;
    In the faith that looks through death,
In years that bring the philosophic mind.

WILLIAM WORDSWORTH
Intimations of Immortality

The Reaper

I am the Reaper.
All things with heedful hook
Silent I gather.
Pale roses touched with spring,
Tall corn in summer,
Fruits rich with autumn, and frail winter blossoms –
All things with heedful hook
Timely I gather.

I am the Sower.
All the unbodied life
Runs through my seed-sheet.
Atom with atom wed,
Each quickening the other,
Fall through my hands, ever changing, still changeless.
Ceaselessly sowing,
Life, incorruptible life,
Flows from my seed-sheet.

Maker and breaker,
I am the ebb and the flood,
Here and Hereafter.
Sped through the tangle and coil
Of infinite nature,
Viewless and soundless I fashion all being.
Taker and giver.
I am the womb and the grave,
The Now and the Ever.

WILLIAM ERNEST HENLEY
Echoes

Facing Change

How do you begin fully to realize that somebody is not there? One important part of the truth is that when you look round for the person you cannot see him or her. At first this just gives you a feeling of puzzlement. Maybe you turn the corner as you come home, and find yourself expecting the person to be at home waiting for you. Maybe you walk into the next room because you thought you heard him or her. Maybe you are watching television, and glance towards his or her usual chair to exchange a smile about something you are enjoying. You expect to see the person, and you find yourself puzzled because you can't.

Your mind then takes the next step – the feeling of puzzlement gives way to one of insecurity. This could take the form of either fear, or anger, or worry. In the early days after bereavement, people find themselves gripped by panic at this point. Their mind rejects the reality, so they can only feel better by feeling that the person will come back soon. But eventually they get past this stage and start to feel less afraid. They still experience fear, anger or worry, but because this is less intense, and because they are learning not to reject the feeling, they can move to the next stage of realization that he or she is not there.

This is the point at which you begin to recognize that the person cannot really be by your side. You search for the face but cannot find it. If this should happen, then you feel a great sense of aloneness, a feeling of being lost and abandoned. This can defeat you too, so you cannot go further with the realization, and relapse into impotent rage at the person for having left you like this, or a terrible fear that you will never survive by yourself. But if it does not defeat you, and you are able to get through the feeling to the other side, you are able to have confidence in your own special qualities – that you have survived before, that you have enough courage, enough resources to get through this time. Then, if you can do this, you will find yourself accepting that he or she is not there, and you will have won for yourself a small part of the total reality of your loss.

DR TONY LAKE
Living with Grief

Shadows

And if tonight my soul may find her peace
in sleep, and sink in good oblivion,
and in the morning wake like a newly opened flower
then I have been dipped again in God, and new-created.

And if, as weeks go round, in the dark of the moon
my spirit darkens and goes out, and soft strange gloom
pervades my movements and my thoughts and words,
then shall I know that I am walking still
with God, we are close together now the moon's in shadow.

And if, as autumn deepens and darkens,
I feel the pain of falling leaves, and stems that break
        in storms
and trouble and dissolution and distress
and then the softness of deep shadows folding, folding
around my soul and spirit, around my lips
so sweet, like a swoon, or more like the drowse of a
        low, dark, song
singing darker than the nightingale, on, on to the
        solstice
and the silence of short days, the silence of the year,
        the shadow.
then I shall know that my life is moving still
with the dark earth, and drenched
with the deep oblivion of earth's lapse and renewal.

And if, in the changing phases of man's life.
I fall in sickness and misery,
my wrists seem broken and my heart seems dead
and strength is gone, and my life
is only the leavings of a life:
and still, among it all, snatches of lovely oblivion, and
        snatches of renewal,
odd, wintry flowers upon the withered stem, yet new,
        strange flowers
such as my life has not brought forth before, new
        blossoms of me,

Then I must know that still
I am in the hands of the unknown God,
he is breaking me down to his own oblivion
to send me forth on a new morning, a new man.

D. H. LAWRENCE
Shadows

The Sequence

And then one or other dies. And we think of this as love
cut short; like a dance stopped in mid career or a flower
with its head unluckily snapped off – something truncated
and therefore, lacking its due shape. I wonder. If, as I can't
help suspecting, the dead also feel the pains of separation
(and this may be one of their purgatorial sufferings), then
for both lovers, and for all pairs of lovers without
exception, bereavement is a universal and integral part of
our experience of love. It follows marriage as normally as
marriage follows courtship or as autumn follows summer.
It is not a truncation of the process but one of its phases;
not the interruption of the dance, but the next figure. We
are "taken out of ourselves" by the loved one while she is
here. Then comes the tragic figure of the dance in which
we must learn to be still taken out of ourselves though the
bodily presence is withdrawn, to love the very Her, and
not fall back to loving our past, or our memory, or our
sorrow, or our relief from sorrow, or our own love.

C. S. LEWIS
A Grief Observed

No Easy Answer

Do not expect, bewildered by your tears,
An easy answer for the heart or mind,
Nor sudden truth to blaze from the unseen,
Nor magic respite from the wound that sears;
To die, that's certain, is to go behind
A wall no eye can pierce, however keen,
A curtain whose divide no hand shall find.

Millions have trusted what the legends tell:
The dead live on, their spirits freed from cares
Beyond our time and skies their pages sing
Throned in pure light or deep in asphodel;
But never witness has returned, who bears
One trophy blossom from that deathless spring,
One sublime phrase of those Elysian airs.

The dead live on: but not in fields of bliss
Where the warm cheek we pressed shall lean again
Welcome to ours beneath the golden bough
And every sorrow vanish in that kiss,
And not with angels, but in the living vein
Of all who sow behind their spirit's plough
And reap in circles the maturing grain;

And though the tears we shed will bring no smile
To lips once set in cold nobility,
It is love's wisdom so to weep, for grief
Can turn the hour of loss from cloudy ill
To that clear element where memory
Throbs like a sun that quickens earth to leaf,
Their simple, mortal immortality.

Only the stabbing moment starts the cry:
"O loved one, whose last words vibrate like bells
Heard over water, you need have no fears,
All shall be done as if you were still by,
All changes eschewed"; but long grief compels
No dedication that may waste our years
Knowing no ghost in watchful sadness dwells.

No ghost shall murmur comfort; therefore, though
If the raw wound shall fester it would seem
Past bearing that one journey never will
Reach harbour where twin hopes had planned to go,
Love's elder faith may cleanse it and redeem
What is no more, from nothing, so it still
Transform the substance of each act and dream. . . .

JOHN LEHMANN
Elegy

Duty

A message came to Joab saying "Behold, the king is weeping and mourning for Absalom." And the victory that day was turned into mourning for all the people, because the people heard it said that day: "The king is grieving for his son." So the people stole into the city that day, just as people who are ashamed steal away when they flee in battle.

Then the king covered his face, and the king cried with a loud voice, "O my son Absalom, O Absalom, my son, my son!"

And Joab came into the house to the king, and said, "You have today covered with shame the faces of all your servants, who have today saved your life, and the lives of your sons and of your daughters, and the lives of your wives, and the lives of your concubines. You love those who hate you and you hate those who love you; for you have shown clearly today that your commanders and your servants are nothing to you; and today I perceive that, if Absalom were alive and all of us were dead today, you would be well pleased. Now therefore arise, go out and make amends to your servants; for I swear by the Lord, if you do not go, not a man will remain with you this night; and that will be worse for you than all the evil which has come upon you from your youth until now."

Then the king arose and took his seat in the gate. And all the people were told "Behold, the king is sitting in the gate"; and all the people came before the king.

2 SAMUEL, XIX

Fortitude

There are certain ladies in our land
Still living and still unafraid
Whose hearts have known a lot of pain,
Whose eyes have shed so many tears,
Who welcomed pity with disdain
And view the fast encroaching years
Humorously and undismayed.

There are certain ladies in our land,
Whose courage is too deeply bred
To merit unreflecting praise.
For them no easy, glib escape;
No mystic hopes confuse their days;
They can identify the shape
Of what's to come, devoid of dread.

There are certain ladies in our land
Who bring to Life the gift of gay
Uncompromising sanity.
The past, for them, is safe and sure.
Perhaps their only vanity
Is that they know they can endure
The rigours of another day.

NOEL COWARD
To L.R-M

Counsel

The world is pitiless and lewdly jeers
All tragedy. Anticipate your loss.
Weep silently, in secret. Hide your tears,
So to become accustomed to your cross.

Alone grief can ennoble us. She only
Is grand and pure. Then learn to love her now –
To be your muse, when you are left and lonely,
And lay the last green laurels on your brow.

She will be sent from Heaven. The seraphic
Language she speaks in, you should learn, for she
Can talk no other in your daily traffic

When you receive her to replace your bride.
Pray humbly, too, to God, that she may be
A constant, kind companion at your side.

ROY CAMPBELL
Counsel

Consolation

Many are the sayings of the wise
In ancient and in modern books enroll'd
Extolling patience as the truest fortitude;
And to the bearing well of all calamities,
All chances incident to man's frail life,
Consolatories writ
With studied argument and much persuasion sought,
Lenient of grief and anxious thought,
But with th'afflicted in his pangs their sound
Little prevails, or rather seems a tune
Harsh, and of dissonant mood from his complaint,
Unless he feel within
Some source of consolation from above;
Secret refreshings that repair his strength
And fainting spirits uphold.

JOHN MILTON
Samson Agonistes

Time's Veil

O time! who know'st a lenient hand to lay
Softest on sorrow's wound, and slowly thence
(Lulling to sad repose the weary sense)
The faint pang stealest unperceived away;
On thee I rest my only hope at last,
And think, when thou hast dried the bitter tear
That flows in vain o'er all my soul held dear,
I may look back on every sorrow past,
And meet life's peaceful evening with a smile:
As some lone bird, at day's departing hour,
Sings in the sunbeam, of the transient shower
Forgetful, though its wings are wet the while:
      Yet ah! how much must this poor heart endure,
      Which hopes from thee, and thee alone, a cure!

WILLIAM LISLE BOWLES

Cold in the earth, and the deep snow piled above thee!
      Far, far removed, cold in the dreary grave!
Have I forgot, my Only Love, to love thee,
      Severed at last by Time's all wearing wave?

Now, when alone, do my thoughts no longer hover
      Over the mountains on Angora's shore,
Resting their wings where heath and fern-leaves cover
      That noble heart for ever, ever more?

Cold in the earth – and fifteen wild Decembers
    From those brown hills have melted into spring –
Faithful indeed is the spirit that remembers
    After such years of change and suffering!

Sweet Love of youth, forgive if I forget thee
    While the world's tide is bearing me along:
Sterner desires and darker hopes beset me,
    Hopes which obscure, but cannot do thee wrong!

No other Sun has lightened up my heaven,
    No other Star has ever shone for me;
All my life's bliss from thy dear life was given,
    All my life's bliss is in the grave with thee.

But when the days of golden dreams had perished
    And even Despair was powerless to destroy,
Then did I learn how existence could be cherished,
    Strengthened and fed without the aid of joy.

Then did I check the tears of useless passion,
    Weaned my young soul from yearning after thine;
Sternly denied its burning wish to hasten
    Down to that tomb already more than mine!

And even yet, I dare not let it languish,
    Dare not indulge in Memory's rapturous pain;
Once drinking deep of that divinest anguish,
    How could I seek the empty world again?

EMILY BRONTE
R. Alcona to J. Brenzaida

The Widower

For a season there must be pain –
For a little, little space
I shall lose the sight of her face,
Take back the old life again
While She is at rest in her place.

For a season this pain must endure,
For a little, little while
I shall sigh more often than smile
Till Time shall work me a cure,
And the pitiful days beguile.

For that season we must be apart,
For a little length of years,
Till my life's last hour nears,
And, above the beat of my heart,
I hear Her voice in my ears.

But I shall not understand –
Being set on some later love,
Shall not know her for whom I strove,
Till she reach me forth her hand,
Saying, "Who but I have the right?"
And out of a troubled night
Shall draw me safe to the land.

RUDYARD KIPLING
The Widower

The Threshold Of The New

The old always gives way and is replaced by the new, and one thing must be made good out of another. There is no dark pit of Hell awaiting anyone. Matter is needed, so that later generations may grow; yet all of them, too, will follow you when they have lived out their span of life. As with you, generations have passed away before, and will do so again. Thus one thing will never cease to arise from another. To none is life given in freehold; to all on lease. Look back at the eternity of time that passed before we were born, and see how utterly unimportant it is to us. Nature holds this up to us as a mirror of the time that is to come after we are dead. Is there anything terrifying in the sight? Anything to grieve over? Is it not a rest more tranquil than any sleep?

LUCRETIUS
The Nature of the Universe

Weep You No More, Sad Fountains

Weep you no more, sad fountains;
What need you flow so fast?
Look how the snowy mountains
Heaven's sun doth gently waste.
But my sun's heavenly eyes
View not your weeping,
That now lies sleeping
Softly, now softly lies
Sleeping.

Sleep is a reconciling,
A rest that peace begets;
Doth not the sun rise smiling
When fair at ev'n he sets?
Rest you then, rest, sad eyes,
Melt not in weeping
While she lies sleeping
Softly, now softly lies
Sleeping.

ANONYMOUS
*from The Third and Last Book of Songs or Aires
by John Dowland*

So Sound You Sleep

The half-moon westers low, my love,
    And the wind brings up the rain;
And wide apart lie we, my love,
    And seas between the twain.

I know not if it rains, my love,
    In the land where you do lie;
And oh, so sound you sleep, my love,
    You know no more than I.

A. E. HOUSMAN

No Longer Mourn For Me

No longer mourn for me when I am dead
Than you should hear the surly sullen bell
Give warning to the world that I am fled
From this vile world, with vilest worms to dwell:
Nay, if you read this line, remember not
The hand that writ it; for I love you so,
That I in your sweet thoughts would be forgot,
If thinking on me then should make you woe.
O, if, I say, you look upon this verse
When I perhaps compounded am with clay,
Do not so much as my poor name rehearse;
But let our love even with my life decay;
     Lest the wise world should look into your moan,
     And mock you with me after I am gone.

WILLIAM SHAKESPEARE
Sonnets 71

The First To Go

If I should go before the rest of you
Break not a flower or inscribe a stone,
Nor when I'm gone speak in a Sunday voice
But be the usual selves that I have known.

> Weep if you must
> Parting is hell,
> But life goes on,
> So sing as well.

JOYCE GRENFELL

When I am dead, my dearest,
> Sing no sad songs for me;
Plant thou no roses at my head,
> Nor shady cypress tree:
Be the green grass above me
> With showers and dewdrops wet;
And if thou wilt, remember,
> And if thou wilt, forget.
I shall not see the shadows,
> I shall not feel the rain;
I shall not hear the nightingale
> Sing on, as if in pain;
And dreaming through the twilight
> That doth not rise nor set,
Haply I may remember,
> And haply may forget.

CHRISTINA ROSSETTI
Song

Late Fragment

And did you get what
you wanted from this life, even so?
I did.
And what did you want?
To call myself beloved, to feel myself
beloved on the earth.

RAYMOND CARVER
A New Path to the Waterfall

The Last Journey

A Sparrow's Flight

"It seems to me, O King," he said "that a comparison such as this may be drawn between the present life of men on earth and that length of time of which we have no knowledge – it is as if, on a winter's night, when you sit at table with your captains and your ministers, a single sparrow were to fly swiftly through the hall. Entering through one door, it immediately flies out through another. While it is within it is untouched by winter's storms. But that brief moment of calm is over in a flash. It returns at once to the winter from which it came and vanishes from your sight. Somewhat like this is the life of man; but of what follows it, or what went before, we are utterly ignorant."

THE VENERABLE BEDE
Ecclesiastical History

Birds flitting in and out of the barn
Bring back an Anglo-Saxon story;
The great wooden hall with long fires down the centre,
Their feet in the rushes, their hands tearing the meat,
Suddenly high above them they notice a swallow enter
From the black storm and zigzag over their heads,
Then out once more into the unknown night;
And that, someone remarks, is the life of man.
But now it is time to sleep; one by one
They rise from the bench and their gigantic shadows
Lurch on the shuddering walls. How can the world
Or the non-world beyond harbour a bird?
They close their eyes that smart from the wood-smoke: how
Can anyone even guess his whence and whither?
This indoor flying makes it seem absurd,
Although it itches and nags and flutters and yearns,
To postulate any other life than now.

LOUIS MACNEICE
Dark Age Glosses

The Soul's Garment

Great Nature she doth clothe the soul within,
A fleshly garment which the Fates do spin.
And when these garments are grown old and bare,
With sickness torn, Death takes them off with care,
And folds them up in peace and quiet rest,
And lays them safe within an earthly chest:
Then scours them, and makes them sweet and clean,
Fit for the soul to wear those clothes again.

MARGARET CAVENDISH, DUCHESS OF NEWCASTLE
Poems and Fancies

All Souls' Day

Be careful, then, and be gentle about death.
For it is hard to die, it is difficult to go through
the door, even when it opens.

And the poor dead, when they have left the walled
and silvery city of the now hopeless body
where are they to go, Oh where are they to go?

They linger in the shadow of the earth.
The earth's long conical shadow is full of souls
that cannot find a way across the sea of change.

Be kind, Oh be kind to your dead
and give them a little encouragement
and help them to build their little ship of death.

For the soul has a long, long journey after death
to the sweet home of pure oblivion.
Each needs a little ship, a little ship
and the proper store of meal for the longest journey.

Oh, from out of your heart
provide for your dead once more, equip them
like departing mariners, lovingly.

D. H. LAWRENCE
All Souls' Day

A Garden By The Sea

I know a little garden-close
Set thick with lily and red rose,
Where I would wander if I might
From dewy morn to dewy night,
And have one with me wandering.

And though within it no birds sing,
And though no pillared house is there,
And though the apple-boughs are bare
Of fruit and blossom, would to God
Her feet upon the green grass trod,
And I beheld them as before.

There comes a murmur from the shore,
And in the close two fair streams are,
Drawn from the purple hills afar,
Drawn down unto the restless sea:
Dark hills whose heath-bloom feeds no bee,
Dark shore no ship has ever seen,
Tormented by the billows green
Whose murmur comes unceasingly
Unto the place for which I cry.
For which I cry both day and night,
For which I let slip all delight,
Whereby I grow both deaf and blind,
Careless to win, unskilled to find,

And quick to lose what all men seek.
Yet tottering as I am and weak,
Still have I left a little breath
To seek within the jaws of death
An entrance to that happy place,
To seek the unforgotten face,
Once seen, once kissed, once reft from me
Anigh the murmuring of the sea.

WILLIAM MORRIS
Poems by the Way

Stay For Me There

Sleep on my Love in thy cold bed
Never to be disquieted!
My last good night! Thou wilt not wake
Till I thy fate shall overtake:
Till age, or grief, or sickness must
Marry my body to that dust
It so much loves; and fill the room
My heart keeps empty in thy tomb.
Stay for me there; I will not fail
To meet thee in that hollow vale.
And think not much of my delay;
I am already on the way,
And follow thee with all the speed
Desire can make, or sorrows breed.
Each minute is a short degree,
And every hour a step towards thee . . .

'Tis true, with shame and grief I yield,
Thou like the van first took the field,
And gotten hast the victory
In thus adventuring to die
Before me, whose more years might crave
A just precedence in the grave.
But hark! My pulse like a soft drum
Beats my approach, tells thee I come;

And slow how'er my marches be,
I shall at last sit down with thee.

HENRY KING, BISHOP OF CHICHESTER
The Exequy

I Shall Find You

In the grey summer garden I shall find you
With day-break and the morning hills behind you.
There will be rain-wet roses; stir of wings;
And down the wood a thrush that wakes and sings.
Not from the past you'll come, but from that deep
Where beauty murmurs to the soul asleep:
And I shall know the sense of life re-born
From dreams into the mystery of morn
Where gloom and brightness meet. And standing there
Till that calm song is done, at last we'll share
The league-spread, quiring symphonies that are
Joy in the world, and peace, and dawn's one star.

SIEGFRIED SASSOON
Idyll

One Another's Mystery

So when from hence we shall be gone,
    And be no more, nor you, nor I
    As one another's mystery
Each shall be both, yet both be one.

LORD HERBERT OF CHERBURY
Whether Love should continue for ever?

They that love beyond the world, cannot be separated.
Death cannot kill what never dies. Nor can Spirits ever be
divided that love and live in the same Divine Principle; the
Root and Record of their Friendship. Death is but crossing
the world, as Friends do the seas; they live in one another
still.

WILLIAM PENN
Fruits of Solitude

I seem to have loved you in numberless forms, numberless times,
In life after life, in age after age forever.
My spell-bound heart has made and re-made the necklace of songs
That you take as a gift, wear round your neck in
                                   your many forms
In life after life, in age after age forever.

Whenever I hear old chronicles of love, its age-old pain,
Its ancient tale of being apart or together,
As I stare on and on into the past, in the end you emerge
Clad in the light of a pole-star piercing the darkness of time:
You become an image of what is remembered forever.

You and I have floated here on the stream that brings from
                                        the fount
At the heart of time love of one for another.
We have played alongside millions of lovers, shared in the same
Shy sweetness of meeting, the same distressful tears of
                                        farewell –
Old love, but in shapes that renew and renew forever.

Today it is heaped at your feet, it has found its end in you,
The love of all man's days both past and forever:
Universal joy, universal sorrow, universal life,
The memories of all loves merging with this one love of ours –
And the songs of every poet past and forever.

RABINDRANATH TAGORE
Manasi
translated by William Radice

Do They Return?

Of apparitions, he (Johnson) observed, "A total disbelief
of them is adverse to the opinion of the existence of the
soul between death and the last day; the question simply
is, whether departed spirits ever have the power of making
themselves perceptible to us; a man who thinks he has
seen an apparition, can only be convinced himself; his
authority will not convince another, and his conviction, if
rational, must be founded upon being told something
which cannot be known but by supernatural means".

SAMUEL JOHNSON
Boswell's Life of Johnson

Why do we return? Not in the darkened rooms
Of rattling tambourines and butter muslin;
But as you boil an egg or make the bed
     You hear us and answer "Darling?"
Yes, that's our wish, after all, whatever ancient
Boredom or intervening cause of unwelcome
Would face us, for our presence once again
     To be taken all for granted.
We don't come in actuality, alas!
For we're in a place that even cosmologists,
Speculating on collapsed stars and anti-matter,
     Couldn't find more alien.

ROY FULLER
The Reign of Sparrows

Don't Be Afraid, I Am With You

The rooms and days we wandered through
Shrink in my mind to one – there you
Lie quite absorbed by peace – the calm
Which life could not provide is balm
In death. Unseen by me, you look
Past bed and stairs and half-read book
Eternally upon your home,
The end of pain, the left alone.
I have no friend, or intercessor,
No psychopomp or true confessor
But only you who know my heart
In every cramped and devious part –
Then take my hand and lead me out,
The sky is overcast by doubt,
The time has come, I listen for
Your words of comfort at the door,
O guide me through the shoals of fear –
"Fürchte dich nicht, ich bin bei dir."*

PETER PORTER
An Exequy

* "Don't be afraid, I am with you." Pamina to Tamino in Mozart's *Magic Flute*.

An Impression

I said, several notebooks ago, that even if I got what
seemed like an assurance of H's presence, I wouldn't
believe it. Easier said than done. Even now, though, I
won't treat anything of that sort as evidence. It's the
quality of last night's experience – not what it proves but
what it was – that makes it worth putting down. It was
quite incredibly unemotional. Just the impression of her
mind momentarily facing my own. Mind, not "soul" as we
tend to think of soul. Certainly the reverse of what is
called "soulful". Not at all like a rapturous re-union of
lovers. Much more like getting a telephone call or a wire
from her about some practical arrangement. Not that there
was any "message" – just intelligence and attention. No
sense of joy or sorrow. No love even, in our ordinary
sense. No un-love. I had never in any mood imagined the
dead as being so – well, so business-like. Yet there was an
extreme and cheerful intimacy. An intimacy that had not
passed through the senses or the emotions at all.

C. S. LEWIS
A Grief Observed

At Daybreak

I listen for him through the rain,
And in the dusk of starless hours
I know that he will come again;
Loth was he ever to forsake me:
He comes with glimmerings of flowers
And stir of music to awake me.

Spirit of purity, he stands
As once he lived in charm and grace;
I may not hold him with my hands,
Nor bid him stay to heal my sorrow;
Only his fair, unshadowed face
Abides with me until to-morrow.

SIEGFRIED SASSOON
Collected Poems

She Comes To Me

She comes not when Noon is on the roses –
    Too bright is Day.
She comes not to the soul till it reposes
    From work and play.

But when Night is on the hills, and the great Voices
    Roll in from Sea
By starlight and by candlelight and dreamlight
    She comes to me.

HERBERT TRENCH

In Every Dream

In every dream thy lovely features rise;
I see them in the sunshine of the day;
Thy form is flitting still before my eyes
Where'er at eve I tread my lonely way;
In every moaning wind I hear thee say
Sweet words of consolation, while thy sighs
Seem borne along on every blast that flies;
I live, I talk with thee where'er I stray:
And yet thou never more shalt come to me
On earth, for thou art in a world of bliss,
And fairer still – if fairer thou canst be –
Than when thou bloomed'st for a while in this.
     Few be my days of loneliness and pain
     Until I meet in love with thee again.

WILLIAM BARNES
Sonnet

Made One With Nature

He is made one with Nature: there is heard
His voice in all her music, from the moan
Of thunder, to the song of night's sweet bird;
He is a presence to be felt and known
In darkness and in light, from herb and stone,
Spreading itself where'er that Power may move
Which has withdrawn its being to his own;
Which wields the world with never-wearied love,
Sustains it from beneath, and kindles it above.

PERCY BYSSHE SHELLEY
Adonais

The Forest

I have come to the borders of sleep,
The unfathomable deep
Forest, where all must lose
Their way, however straight
Or winding, soon or late;
They cannot choose.

Many a road and track
That since the dawn's first crack
Up to the forest brink
Deceived the travellers,
Suddenly now blurs,
And in they sink.

Here love ends –
Despair, ambition ends;
All pleasure and all trouble,
Although most sweet or bitter,
Here ends, in sleep that is sweeter
Than tasks most noble.

There is not any book
Or face of dearest look
That I would not turn from now
To go into the unknown
I must enter, and leave, alone,
I know not how.

The tall forest towers:
Its cloudy foliage lowers
Ahead, shelf above shelf;
Its silence I hear and obey
That I may lose my way
And myself.

EDWARD THOMAS
Lights Out

Up-Hill

Does the road wind up-hill all the way?
>Yes, to the very end.
Will the day's journey take the whole long day?
>From morn to night, my friend.

But is there for the night a resting-place?
>A roof for when the slow dark hours begin.
May not the darkness hide it from my face?
>You cannot miss that inn.

Shall I meet other wayfarers at night?
>Those who have gone before.
Then must I knock, or call when just in sight?
>They will not keep you standing at that door.

Shall I find comfort, travel-sore and weak?
>Of labour you shall find the sum.
Will there be beds for me and all who seek?
>Yea, beds for all who come.

CHRISTINA ROSSETTI
Up-Hill

A New Dawn

'Tis but a night, a long and moonless night,
We make the Grave our bed, and then are gone.
Thus at the shut of ev'n, the weary bird
Leaves the wide air, and in some lonely brake
Cow'rs down, and dozes till the dawn of day,
Then claps his well-fledg'd wings, and bears away . . .

ROBERT BLAIR
The Grave

The Last Day

Behold, I shew you a mystery: We shall not all sleep, but
we shall all be changed, in a moment, in the twinkling of
an eye, at the last trump. For the trumpet shall sound, and
the dead shall be raised incorruptible, and we shall be
changed. For this corruptible must put on incorruption,
and this mortal must put on immortality. So when this
corruptible shall have put on incorruption, and this mortal
shall have put on immortality, then shall be brought to
pass the saying that is written: Death is swallowed up in
victory. O death, where is thy sting? O grave, where is
thy victory?

I CORINTHIANS, XV. 51
Epistle of the First Mass for All Souls Day

Death, Be Not Proud

Death, be not proud, though some have called thee
Mighty and dreadful, for thou art not so;
For those whom thou think'st thou dost overthrow
Die not, poor Death; nor yet canst thou kill me.
From rest and sleep, which but thy pictures be,
Much pleasure; then from thee much more must flow;
And soonest our best men with thee do go –
Rest of their bones, and soul's delivery!
Thou'rt slave to fate, chance, kings, and desperate men,
And dost with poison, war, and sickness dwell;
And poppy or charms can make us sleep as well
And better than thy stroke. Why swell'st thou then?
One short sleep past, we wake eternally,
And Death shall be no more: Death, thou shalt die!

JOHN DONNE
Divine Poems

Christ's Promise

Then Martha said to Jesus: "Lord, if you had been here my brother would not have died. But I know that even now, whatever you may ask of God, God will grant it to you."

Jesus says to her: "Your brother will rise again."

Martha says to him: "I know that he will rise again, in the resurrection when the last day comes."

Jesus said to her: "I am the resurrection and life. He who believes in me, though he is dead, will live. And everyone who lives, and believes in me, to eternity will never die. Do you believe this?"

"Yes, Lord," she replied. "I have grown to believe that you are the Christ, the Son of God, who comes into the world."

JOHN, VIII. 21
The Gospel of the Mass for the Dead

An End To Tears

And God shall wipe away all tears from their eyes;
    and there shall be no more death, neither sorrow,
    nor crying, neither shall there be any more pain:
    for the former things are passed away.

THE REVELATION OF ST JOHN THE DIVINE
XXI. 4

Acknowledgements

BERRYMAN, John. "An Empty Heart" (He Resigns) from *Collected Poems of John Berryman 1937–1971*, published by Faber and Faber Ltd. Copyright © Kate Donohue Berryman 1989. Reprinted by permission of Faber and Faber Ltd.

BETJEMAN, John. "House of Rest" from *Collected Poems*, published by John Murray (Publishers) Ltd. Copyright © Estate of John Betjeman 1989. Reprinted by permission of John Murray (Publishers) Ltd.

CAMPBELL, Roy. "Do this Favour for me" (translation) and "Counsel", from *The Collected Poems of Roy Campbell*, published by The Bodley Head Ltd, London. Copyright Estate of Roy Campbell.

CARVER, Raymond. "No Need" and "Late Fragment" from *A New Path to the Waterfall*, published by Collins Harvill. Copyright © Estate of Raymond Carver 1989. Reprinted by permission of HarperCollins*Publishers* and Atlantic Monthly Press.

CAVAFY, C. P. "Voices" from *The Complete Poems of C. P. Cavafy*, translated by Rae Dalven and published by the Hogarth Press Ltd. Copyright Estate of C. P. Cavafy. Reprinted by permission of Random Century Ltd.

CORNFORD, Frances. "All Souls' Night" from *Collected Poems of Frances Cornford*, published by Hutchinson. Copyright Estate of Frances Cornford. Reprinted by permission of Random Century Ltd.

COWARD, Noel. "Fortitude" (To L.R-M) from *The Collected Verse of Noel Coward*, published by Methuen London. Copyright Estate of Noel Coward. Reprinted by permission of Methuen London.

DE LA MARE, Walter. "The Widow" and "Love lies here" from *Collected Poems*, published by Faber and Faber Ltd. Copyright © Literary Trustees of Walter De la Mare 1979. Reprinted by permission of The Society of Authors as their representative.

DRAYCOTT, Jane. "Search" from *Braving the Dark*. Copyright © Jane Draycott 1992.

DUNN, Douglas. "Summer" (France) and "The Kaleidoscope" from *Selected Poems 1964–1983*, published by Faber and Faber Ltd. Copyright © Douglas Dunn 1986. Reprinted by permission of Faber and Faber Ltd.

FULLER, Roy. "Do they return?" from *New and Collected Poems* published by Martin Secker and Warburg Ltd. Copyright © Estate of Roy Fuller 1985. Reprinted by permission of Martin Secker and Warburg Ltd.

GRAVES, Robert. "Pure Death" from *Collected Poems 1975*, published by Cassell plc. Copyright © The Trustees of the Robert Graves Copyright Trust 1975. Reprinted by permission of A. P. Watt Ltd. and Oxford University Press Inc.

GRENFELL, Joyce. "The First to go" from *Joyce – By Herself and Her Friends*, published by Macmillan Ltd. Copyright © The Joyce Grenfell Memorial Trust 1980. Reprinted by permission of Richard Scott Simon Ltd. on behalf of the Trustees.

HAILSHAM OF ST MARYLEBONE, Lord. "If Grief could burn out" from *A Sparrow's Flight*, published by Fontana. Copyright © Lord Hailsham of St Marylebone 1989. Reprinted by permission of HarperCollins*Publishers*.

KAVANAGH, Patrick. "A Memory of his Mother" from *Collected Poems*, published by Longman Green & Co.

LAKE, Dr Tony. "Facing Change" from *Living with Grief*, published by the Sheldon Press. Copyright © Dr Tony Lake 1984. Reprinted by permission of the Sheldon Press.

LARKIN, Philip. "Home is so Sad", "On Wakening" and "If Grief could burn out" from *Collected Poems*, published by Faber and Faber Ltd. Copyright © The Estate of Philip Larkin 1988. Reprinted by permission of Faber and Faber Ltd.

LEHMANN, John. "No Easy Answer" (Elegy) from *The Age of the Dragon: Poems 1930–1951*, published by Longman Green & Co. Copyright Estate of John Lehmann. Reprinted by permission of David Higham Associates Ltd on behalf of the Estate.

LEWIS, C. S. "Grief's Circle", "The Sequence" and "An Impression" from *A Grief Observed*, published by Faber and Faber Ltd. Copyright © 1961 by N. W. Clerk. Reprinted by permission of Faber and Faber Ltd.

LEWIS, C. S. "Joys once shared" from *Poems*, published by Collins Publishers. Copyright Estate of C. S. Lewis. Reprinted by permission of HarperCollins*Publishers*.

MACNEICE, Louis. "A Sparrow's Flight" from *The Collected Poems of Louis MacNeice*, published by Faber and Faber Ltd. Copyright © Estate of Louis MacNeice 1966. Reprinted by permission of Faber and Faber Ltd.

MILLAY, Edna St Vincent. "Now sits the autumn cricket in the grass" and the sestet from "Time does not bring relief" from *Collected Poems*, published by HarperCollins. Copyright © Edna St Vincent Millay and Norma Millay Ellis 1917, 1945, 1954, 1982. Reprinted by permission of Elizabeth Barnett, literary executor.

O'CONNOR, Frank. "Half of Me" (translation) from *The Faber Book of Irish Verse*, published by Faber and Faber Ltd. Reprinted by permission of Peters Fraser & Dunlop Group Ltd.

PARTRIDGE, Frances. "My Days go on" from *Hanging On*, published by William Collins Sons and Co. Ltd. Copyright © Frances Partridge 1989. Reprinted by permission of HarperCollins*Publishers* and Rogers, Coleridge & White Ltd.

PORTER, Peter. "A Card comes" (Non piangere liù) and "Don't be afraid, I am with you" (Exequy) from *Collected Poems*, published by the Oxford University Press. Copyright © Peter Porter 1989. Reprinted by permission of the Oxford University Press.

POWYS, John Cowper. "Nunc Dimittis" from *Mandragora*, published by Village Press Ltd. Copyright Estate of John Cowper Powys. Reprinted by permission of Laurence Pollinger Ltd.

PROUST, Marcel. "My True Love hath my Heart" (translation) from *Remembrance of Things Past*, translated by C. K. Scott Moncrieff and published by Chatto & Windus Ltd.

RADICE, William. "One Another's Mystery" (Unending Love) (translation) from *Rabindranath Tagore: Selected Poems*, translated by William Radice and published by Penguin Books. Copyright © William Radice 1985. Reprinted by permission of Penguin Books Ltd.

SASSOON, Siegfried. "When I'm alone", "I shall find you" and "At Daybreak" from *Collected Poems 1908–1956*, published by Faber and Faber Ltd. Copyright Estate of Siegfried Sassoon. Reprinted by permission of George Sassoon.

SIMPSON, Louis. "Whispers" from *Collected Poems of Louis Simpson*, published by Paragon House. Copyright © Louis Simpson 1988. Reprinted by permission of Paragon House.

SYMONS, Arthur. "When you were here" and "That Tune" from *Collected Poems*, published by William Heinemann & Co. Copyright Literary Executor of Arthur Symons. Reprinted by permission of Brian Read.

WADDELL, Helen. "Thee shall I hold" (translation) from *Mediaeval Latin Lyrics*, translated by Helen Waddell and published by Penguin Books Ltd. Reprinted by permission of Constable & Co. Ltd. and Miss Mary Martin.

WALKER, Ted. "Home is so sad" from *The Last of England*, published by Jonathan Cape. Copyright © Ted Walker 1992. Reprinted by permission of David Higham Associates.

While every effort has been made to secure permission, it has in some cases proved impossible to trace the copyright holder. I must apologize if any inadvertent omission has occurred.

Index of First Lines of Verse

Index of Authors